FREE DVD  **FREE DVD**

Wonderlic DVD from Trivium Test Prep!

Dear Customer,

Thank you for purchasing from Trivium Test Prep! We're honored to help you prepare for your AP exam.

To show our appreciation, we're offering a **FREE** *Wonderlic Essential Test Tips* **DVD by Trivium Test Prep**. Our DVD includes 35 test preparation strategies that will make you successful on the AP Exam. All we ask is that you email us your feedback and describe your experience with our product. Amazing, awful, or just so-so: we want to hear what you have to say!

To receive your **FREE** *Wonderlic Essential Test Tips* **DVD**, please email us at 5star@triviumtestprep.com. Include "Free 5 Star" in the subject line and the following information in your email:

1. The title of the product you purchased.

2. Your rating from 1 – 5 (with 5 being the best).

3. Your feedback about the product, including how our materials helped you meet your goals and ways in which we can improve our products.

4. Your full name and shipping address so we can send your **FREE** *Wonderlic Essential Test Tips* **DVD**.

If you have any questions or concerns please feel free to contact us directly at 5star@triviumtestprep.com. Thank you!

- Trivium Test Prep Team

Table of Contents

Introduction

Although the Wonderlic Test is famous for its use in the NFL (and for some of the infamously poor scores attained on it by famous athletes), it is also used by employers to evaluate potential employees.

Good news: There is no passing or failing on this test! Instead, employers have their own separate requirements for achievement standards. Make sure to check! Remember, you are presenting yourself as a potential employee – you want to put your best foot forward; and that means getting a good score.

To do well on the Wonderlic, you must possess a basic knowledge of math and vocabulary through the 9th or 10th grade level. You must also be familiar with standard information such as how many days are in a year, how many weeks are in a year, etc.

The questions are not separated into different sections – such as Math, Reading, or Science – like on other standardized exams. Instead, all questions are mixed together, and many will include reading comprehension, vocabulary, and mathematics in a single question.

Breaking Down the Test

The Basic Skills Test is broken into two sections:

- **Verbal Skills**: 20-minute time limit; 50 questions.

  These questions will test your knowledge of vocabulary words, as well as sentence structure, grammar, and usage.

- **Quantitative Skills**: 20-minute time limit; 45 questions.

  These questions will test your mathematical knowledge through the 10th grade level. Questions will be presented as both numerical math problems as well as word problems.

Depending on your potential employer's requirements, you may be administered only one of these sections. Make sure to check!

How to Study

When studying for the Wonderlic exam, you shouldn't try to tackle everything at once (no pun intended). Instead, it is vitally important to get back to the basics. Work on the fundamentals first; then you can recall that information as needed on the actual exam.

Chapter 1: Quantitative Skills

In the following practice test, be sure to take it in realistic conditions: time yourself, do not cheat by going over the time limit. Remember, this practice is for you, not anyone else. Use this as an opportunity to improve and evaluate where you might need more work.

1. You have $20 to buy sandals that cost $10 in a state with 8% sales tax. How much will you pay?
   a) $18.00.
   b) $10.80.
   c) $8.10.
   d) $20.08.
   e) $18.1.

2. If a wheel spins at 30 rpm (revolutions per minute), how long will it take for the wheel to spin 45 times?
   a) 5 minutes.
   b) 1 minutes.
   c) 3 minutes.
   d) .5 minute.
   e) 1.5 minutes.

3. A Coke can is 5 inches long; if you stack Coke cans end to end, what is the maximum number of cans you can fit in a length of 4 feet?
   a) 4 cans.
   b) 50 cans.
   c) 5 cans.
   d) 9 cans.
   e) 18 cans.

4. With the same 5" Coke cans, how long would 8 cans stacked end to end be?
   a) 40 inches.
   b) 2 feet.
   c) 8 inches.
   d) 16 inches.
   e) 22 inches.

5. A book is sitting on the carpet. Which force resists you trying to slide the book across the floor?
   a) Inertia.
   b) Gravity.
   c) Momentum.
   d) Friction.

6. 1 pound equals 16 ounces. In terms of pounds, how much is 4 ounces?
   a) 2 pounds.
   b) .25 pounds.
   c) .5 pounds.
   d) 0.49 pounds.
   e) 3 pounds.

7. What is 705.201718 rounded to the nearest tenth?
    a) 705.2.
    b) 705.
    c) 705.1.
    d) 706.
    e) 707.2.

8. What is 211.8714 rounded to the nearest whole number?
    a) 212.
    b) 210.
    c) 200.
    d) 211.8.
    e) 2118714.

9. Round 17.1298 to the nearest hundredths place.
    a) 18.
    b) 17.1.
    c) 17.13.
    d) 17.9.
    e) 17.

10. What is the average of 2, 3, 15, and 20?
    a) 10.
    b) 5.
    c) 20.
    d) 3.
    e) 18.

11. What is the average of 10, 6, 14, 8, and 2?
    a) 8.
    b) 14.
    c) 3.
    d) 19.
    e) 30.

12. What is the mode of the following numbers: 4, 5, 6, 7, 7, 8, 9, 4, 10, 11, 4?
    a) 5.
    b) 6.
    c) 4.
    d) 7.
    e) 10.

13. What is the mode of the following numbers: 220, 122, 220, 410, 244, 220, 122?
    a) 122.
    b) 244.
    c) 410.
    d) 220.
    e) 210.

14. Add 1.07 + 6.817 + 30.915.
   a) 60.27.
   b) 38.802.
   c) 16.716.
   d) 48.73.
   e) 34.719.

15. Add 11.6517 + 4.37 + 0.965.
   a) 12.4745.
   b) 22.3896.
   c) 16.9867.
   d) 21.1619.
   e) 22.1717.

16. Add 22.1716 + 0.16 + 4.297.
   a) 23.7446.
   b) 31.0457.
   c) 26.6286.
   d) 33.1658.
   e) 36.2837.

17. Multiply 18 * 0.1.
   a) 18.1.
   b) 1.8.
   c) 8.18.
   d) 0.018.
   e) 180.

18. Multiply 200 * 5.5
   a) 2,500.
   b) 255.5.
   c) 1,100.
   d) 11,000.
   e) 520.

19. Multiply 22 * 0.5.
   a) 44.
   b) 33.
   c) 11.
   d) 18.
   e) 28.

20. Multiply 40 * 0.25.
   a) 60.
   b) 4.
   c) 22.
   d) 10.
   e) 80.

21. -47 + 5 equals:
   a) 42.
   b) -42.
   c) 52.
   d) -52.
   e) -5.

22. -32 + 6 equals:
   a) 26.
   b) -26.
   c) 38.
   d) -38.
   e) -32.6.

23. -52 + 16 equals:
   a) 68.
   b) -68.
   c) -36.
   d) 36.
   e) 14.

24. 0.52 equals which of the following:
   a) 52%.
   b) 520%.
   c) 5.2%.
   d) 2.55%.
   e) 525%.

25. 47% equals which of the following:
   a) .47.
   b) 47.
   c) 1.47.
   d) 470.
   e) 4.7.

26. 0.99 equals which of the following:
   a) 9.9%.
   b) 99%.
   c) 999%.
   d) 1.9%.
   e) 199%.

27. Which of the following is the largest number?
   a) 15.
   b) 1.555.
   c) 1500.
   d) 150.550.
   e) 15.55.

28. Which of the following is the smallest number?
  a) .01.
  b) 1.10.
  c) 1.
  d) .111.
  e) 11.1.

29. Which of the following is the smallest number?
  a) 5.52.
  b) .552.
  c) 552.
  d) 55.2.
  e) 2.55.

30. What is the next number in the sequence: 2, 4, 8, 16, ___?
  a) 24.
  b) 32.
  c) 48.
  d) 18.
  e) 42.

31. What is the next number in the sequence: 3, 6, 9, 12, 15, ___?
  a) 18.
  b) 30.
  c) 33.
  d) 29.
  e) 16.

32. What is the next number in the sequence: 4, 8, 12, 16, ___?
  a) 18.
  b) 17.
  c) 20.
  d) 30.
  e) 32.

33. Approximately how many days have passed in the calendar year on December 1st (this is not a leap year)?
  a) 255.
  b) 334.
  c) 358.
  d) 280.
  e) 150.

34. What is the average number of weeks in a month?
  a) 4.3.
  b) 5.3.
  c) 3.5.
  d) 6.
  e) 3.

35. The 10th month of the year is:
   a) December.
   b) May.
   c) August.
   d) October.
   e) January.

36. If 2 cups equals 1 pint, how many cups are in 3 pints?
   a) 8.
   b) 3.
   c) 2.
   d) 6.
   e) 10.

37. How many inches are in 3.5 feet?
   a) 30.
   b) 24.
   c) 42.
   d) 60.
   e) 16.

38. How many millimeters are in 2 meters?
   a) 200.
   b) 2,000,000.
   c) 2,000.
   d) 20.
   e) 2.

39. What will it cost to carpet a room with indoor/outdoor carpet if the room is 10 feet wide and 12 feet long? The carpet costs $12.51 per square yard.
   a) $166.80
   b) $175.90
   c) $184.30
   d) $189.90
   e) $192.20

40. Edmond has to sell his BMW. He bought the car for $49,000, but sold it at 20% less. At what price did Edmond sell the car?
   a) $24,200
   b) $28,900
   c) $35,600
   d) $37,300
   e) $39,200

Quantitative Skills Practice Test – Answers

1. b)	21. b)
2. e)	22. b)
3. d)	23. c)
4. a)	24. a)
5. d)	25. a)
6. b)	26. b)
7. a)	27. c)
8. a)	28. a)
9. c)	29. b)
10. a)	30. b)
11. a)	31. a)
12. c)	32. c)
13. d)	33. b)
14. b)	34. a)
15. c)	35. d)
16. c)	36. d)
17. b)	37. c)
18. c)	38. c)
19. c)	39. a)
20. d)	40. e)

Chapter 2: Verbal Skills Practice Test

In the following practice test, be sure to take it in realistic conditions: time yourself and do not cheat by going over the time limit. Remember, this practice is for you, not anyone else. Use this as an opportunity to improve and evaluate where you might need more work.

For questions 1 – 10, select the best segment to replace the underlined segment of the sentence.

1. Rod cells are found in the human <u>eye so they can absorb light to see in even dim environments</u>.
   a) "eye, but can absorb light to see in even dim environments."
   b) "eye to see in dim environments even by absorbing light."
   c) "eye and can absorb light to see in even dim environments."
   d) "eye and are absorbing light to see in even dim environments."
   e) "eye so they can absorb light to see in even dim environments."

2. Having already finished her essay, <u>washing the truck was the thing Maricela was ready to do</u>.
   a) "washing the truck was the next thing Maricela did."
   b) "Maricela had another thing she was ready to do and that was washing the truck."
   c) "washing the truck Maricela was ready to do."
   d) "Maricela was ready to wash the truck."
   e) "washing the truck was the thing Maricela was ready to do."

3. The information gathered from the national census <u>is used to determine political boundaries, inform policies, and planning transportation systems</u>.
   a) "is used to determine political boundaries, inform policies, and plan transportation systems."
   b) "determines political boundaries and informs policies and plans transportation systems."
   c) "is determining political boundaries, informing policies, and planning transportation systems."
   d) "is used to determine political boundaries, informing policies, and planning transportation systems."
   e) "is used to determine political boundaries, inform policies, and planning transportation systems."

4. Many artists and producers disagree over how copyright laws <u>should be applied, they have different perspectives</u> on what best protects and encourages creativity.
   a) "should be applied since it is that they have different perspectives"
   b) "are applied with different perspectives"
   c) "should apply on differing perspectives"
   d) "are applied, because they have different perspectives"
   e) "should be applied, they have different perspectives"

5. Many consider television shows <u>to be eroding of our nation's imaginations and attention spans</u>.
   a) "to have eroded our nation's imaginations and attention spans."
   b) "erosion of our nation's imaginations and attention spans."
   c) "to be eroding of our national imaginations and attention spans."
   d) "to be eroding of the national imagination and attention span."
   e) "eroded our nation's imaginations and attention spans."

6. In the early 1960's, the Civil Rights movement in the United States <u>has swiftly grown to encompass</u> such movements as the Freedom Rides and the integration of universities.
   a) "has grown swiftly to encompass"
   b) "has swiftly grown, encompassing"
   c) "growing swiftly has encompassed"
   d) "had swiftly grown to encompass"
   e) "has swiftly grown to encompass"

7. Raul, the most knowledgeable of us all regarding physics, <u>maintain that we would be needing</u> better equipment.
   a) "maintaining that we would need"
   b) "maintains that we would be needing"
   c) "maintains that we would need"
   d) "maintain we would have needed"
   e) "maintain that we would be needing"

8. <u>Does anyone have an informed guess that they would like</u> to share before I reveal the answer?
   a) "Do anyone have an informed guess that they would like"
   b) "Is anyone having an informed guess that they would like"
   c) "Does anyone have an informed guess that they have wanting"
   d) "Anyone with an informed guess would like"
   e) "Does anyone have an informed guess that they would like"

9. <u>The meals at this restaurant have so much more salt in them than the restaurant we went to last week.</u>
   a) "The meals at this restaurant have so much more salt in them than that other restaurant."
   b) "The meals at this restaurant are so much saltier than the restaurant we went to last week."
   c) "The meals at this restaurant have much more salt in them than the restaurant we went to last week."
   d) "The meals at this restaurant have so much more salt in them than those at the restaurant we went to last week."
   e) "The meals at this restaurant have so much more salt in them than the restaurant we went to last week."

10. The Bernina Range <u>runs along eastern Switzerland and is considered to be a part of the</u> Central Eastern Alps.
   a) "is running along eastern Switzerland and is considered to be a part of the"
   b) "runs along eastern Switzerland and is considered part of"
   c) "run along eastern Switzerland, consider to be a part of the"
   d) "run along eastern Switzerland and is considered to be a part of the"
   e) "runs along eastern Switzerland and is considered to be a part of the"

For the following questions, select which of the underlined selections are incorrect within the sentence.

11. When cooking with hot <u>oil, it is prudent</u> for <u>one to wear</u> long sleeves so that want the oil does not <u>splatter onto</u> your arms and burn <u>them</u>.
    a) "oil, it is prudent"
    b) "one to wear"
    c) "splatter onto"
    d) "them."
    e) No error.

12. <u>Jordan and I</u> practiced our show <u>over and over;</u> we <u>would have</u> only twenty minutes to play, and we wanted to make sure <u>to play</u> our best songs.
    a) "Jordan and I"
    b) "over and over;"
    c) "would have"
    d) "to play"
    e) No error.

13. Aliyah asked <u>Timothy and I</u> to help her run the student <u>election;</u> so this week <u>we are hanging</u> posters, printing the ballots, <u>and editing speeches</u>.
    a) "Timothy and I"
    b) "election"
    c) "we are hanging"
    d) "and editing speeches."
    e) No error.

14. The difficulty with navigating <u>subway systems</u> <u>are compounded</u> <u>when some</u> stations are closed for <u>repair</u>.
    a) "subway systems"
    b) "are compounded"
    c) "when some"
    d) "repair."
    e) No error.

15. We <u>were given</u> explicit instructions for how to deal with <u>this exact</u> situation: we are to <u>immediately halt</u> production <u>and be contacting</u> the supervisor.
    a) "were given"
    b) "this exact"
    c) "to immediately halt"
    d) "and be contacting"
    e) No error.

16. The way the <u>shadows play</u> across the leaves <u>provide the artist</u> with <u>innumerable</u> challenges in painting the <u>twilit landscape</u>.
    a) "shadows play"
    b) "provide the artist"
    c) "innumerable"
    d) "the twilit landscape"
    e) No error.

17. <u>Along the banks</u> of the Colorado River <u>grow many different kinds</u> of bushes and trees <u>which serve</u> as habitats for the deer mice, raccoons, jackrabbits, and toads <u>that live there</u>.
    a) "Along the banks"
    b) "grow many different kinds"
    c) "which serve"
    d) "that live there"
    e) No error.

18. Gerald <u>slung his arm</u> about me <u>very</u> <u>familiar, although</u> we had <u>only met hours ago</u>.
    a) "slung his arm"
    b) "very"
    c) "familiar, although"
    d) "only met hours ago"
    e) No error.

19. After hiking <u>all afternoon</u> in the rocky desert, <u>we had</u> a desperate <u>need of</u> water bottles and <u>long, soothing showers</u>.
    a) "all afternoon"
    b) "we had"
    c) "need of"
    d) "long, soothing showers"
    e) No error.

20. It took nearly <u>half an hour</u> to dish out the meals to the large group. First, we had to <u>give everyone food</u>, and then we had to make sure <u>that everyone got</u> <u>their beverage</u> as well.
    a) "half an hour"
    b) "give everyone food"
    c) "that everyone got"
    d) "their beverage"
    e) No error.

21. When considering <u>what kind of</u> car to purchase, it is important to <u>factor in hidden costs</u> such as how much gas <u>the car consumed</u> and how expensive <u>maintenance will be</u>.
    a) "what kind of"
    b) factor in hidden costs"
    c) "the car consumed
    d) "maintenance will be"
    e) No error.

22. Just before <u>the guests arrived</u> Sarah realized that <u>we were going</u> to run out of paper plates, so <u>her and David</u> went to the store to buy <u>some</u>.
    a) "the guests arrived"
    b) "we were going"
    c) "her and David"
    d) "some"
    e) No error.

23. <u>Regardless by</u> how much one <u>likes or appreciates</u> a gift, it is <u>absolutely necessary</u> to thank the giver in person, by telephone, <u>or even with</u> a card.
    a) "Regardless by"
    b) "likes or appreciates"
    c) "absolutely necessary"
    d) "or even with"
    e) No error.

24. Even though Alaina <u>was generally cautious</u> when it came to daring physical feats, she was excited <u>to try</u> spelunking for the first time; <u>she'd heard</u> that <u>the caves were</u> breathtaking.
    a) "was generally cautious"
    b) "to try"
    c) "she'd heard"
    d) "the caves were"
    e) No error.

25. The <u>borders of</u> Rasco County <u>is comprised</u> of the river to the north <u>and east</u> and interstates <u>along the south</u> and the west.
    a) "borders of"
    b) "is comprised"
    c) "and east"
    d) "along the south"
    e) No error.

26. Each <u>applicant for</u> the open time slot <u>was asked</u> to give <u>his opinion on</u> the best way to improve the radio <u>station's programming</u>.
    a) "applicant for"
    b) "was asked"
    c) "his opinion on"
    d) "station's programming"
    e) No error.

27. There <u>will likely never</u> be a general <u>consensus on</u> which <u>is best</u>: the sunrise <u>or</u> the sunset.
    a) "will likely never"
    b) "consensus on"
    c) "is best'
    d) "or"
    e) No error.

28. The storm drew <u>menacing</u> near the town <u>where</u> citizens <u>had been</u> warned to move down to <u>their</u> cellars.
   a) "menacing"
   b) "where"
   c) "had been"
   d) "their"
   e) No error.

29. There are some difficulties inherent <u>for moving</u> across the country. <u>One must</u> secure housing <u>remotely</u> and <u>transport</u> belongings great distances.
   a) "for moving"
   b) "One must"
   c) "remotely"
   d) "transport"
   e) No error.

30. <u>When driving</u> on a <u>major</u> road, <u>to have gone</u> the speed limit <u>is prudent</u>.
   a) "When driving"
   b) "major"
   c) "to have gone"
   d) "is prudent"
   e) No error.

31. Salvador <u>and me</u>, <u>who take</u> Spanish class <u>together</u>, often study in the library <u>prior to</u> exams.
   a) "and me"
   b) "who take"
   c) "together"
   d) "prior to"
   e) No error.

32. <u>Because of</u> the stringent law <u>enacted in</u> the state, legislators <u>must be careful</u> to review <u>policies</u>.
   a) "Because of"
   b) "enacted in"
   c) "must be careful"
   d) "policies"
   e) No error.

33. <u>If the candidate</u> the company <u>had endorsed</u> were <u>to win</u>, the CEO <u>is very</u> pleased.
   a) "If the candidate"
   b) "had endorsed"
   c) "to win"
   d) "is very"
   e) No error.

34. <u>Even though</u> we <u>already understood</u> the solution, the tutor <u>insisted on</u> explaining the steps again to Sara <u>and I</u>.
- a) "Even though"
- b) "already understood"
- c) "insisted on"
- d) "and I"
- e) No error.

35. It is essential to <u>applying</u> the <u>criteria</u> uniformly across all of the candidates <u>in order to</u> judge the contest <u>fairly</u>.
- a) "applying"
- b) "criteria"
- c) "in order to"
- d) "fairly"
- e) No error.

For the following questions, rewrite the sentence in your mind using the provided start of the sentence, then choose the correct answer for what should follow.

36. Ice, which expands when frozen, will take up more space within the container holding it.

Rewrite, beginning with: <u>Expanding when frozen,</u>

The next words will be:

- a) "the container holding it"
- b) "take up more space"
- c) "space is taken"
- d) "ice will take up"
- e) "holding it"

37. Michael, John, and Jerry all enjoy playing football on warm summer mornings if they can find a team to join them.

Rewrite, beginning with: <u>On warm summer mornings,</u>

The next words will be:

- a) "Michael, John, and Jerry"
- b) "playing football"
- c) "enjoy the playing of"
- d) "finding a team to join them"
- e) "the team that joins them"

38. The office party was a success, everyone agreed happily, especially because of the good food.
Rewrite, beginning with: <u>Especially because of the good food,</u>

The next words will be:

a) "agreed"
b) "happily agreed"
c) "a success"
d) "the office"
e) "everyone agreed"

39. Dogs are faithful companions, and can be great addition to any family; but not all dogs are well-suited for hunting and outdoor activities.

Rewrite, beginning with: <u>A great addition to any family,</u>

The next words will be:

a) "All dogs"
b) "dogs are faithful"
c) "companions are"
d) "my dog is black"
e) "hunting and outdoor"

40. Jill was excited after finally learning how to ride a bike.

Rewrite, beginning with: <u>Finally learning how to ride a bike</u>

The next words will be:

a) "was excited"
b) "afterwards Jill"
c) "she was riding"
d) "excited Jill"
e) "finally excited"

Verbal Skills Practice Test – Answers

1. c)
Wordiness and precision.

2. d)
Misplaced modifier and wordiness.

3. a)
Parallelism in listing, subject/verb agreement.

4. d)
Word usage.

5. a)
Verb tense.

6. d)
Verb tense.

7. c)
Subject/verb agreement and gerund use.

8. e)
No error.

9. d)
Imprecise comparisons.

10. e)
No error.

11. b)
"One" and "you" cannot both be used as forms of address in the same sentence.

12. e)
No error.

13. a)
Subject/object pronoun use ("Timothy and me").

14. b)
Subject/verb agreement ("Difficulty is compounded")

15. d)
Parallelism ("and contact")

16. b)
Subject/verb agreement ("The way…provides the artist").

17. e)
No error.

18. c)
Adjective/adverb use ("familiarly although").

19. c)
Proper idiomatic usage ("need for").

20. d)
Subject/verb agreement ("everyone got his or her beverage").

21. c)
Verb tense ("the car will consume").

22. c)
Subject/object pronoun ("David and she went to the store").

23. a)
Proper idiomatic usage ("Regardless of").

24. e)
No error.

25. b)
Subject/verb agreement ("are comprised").

26. c)
Pronoun agreement ("his or her opinion").

27. c)
Superlative use ("is better," since only two things are being compared).

28. a)

Adjective/adverb use ("menacingly").

29. a)

Idiomatic usage ("inherent in/to moving").

30. c)

Verb tense ("going").

31. a)

Subject/object pronoun use ("and I").

32. e)

No error.

33. d)

Verb tense/subjunctive ("would be very").

34. d)

Subject/object pronoun use ("and me").

35. a)

Verb tense ("apply").

36. d)

37. a)

38. e)

39. b)

40. d)

Final Thoughts

In the end, we know that you will be successful in taking the Wonderlic. Although the road ahead may at times be challenging, if you continue your hard work and dedication (just like you are doing to prepare right now!), you will find that your efforts will pay off.

If you are struggling after reading this book and following our guidelines, we sincerely hope that you will take note of our advice and seek additional help. Start by asking friends about the resources that they are using. If you are still not reaching the score you want, consider getting the help of a Wonderlic tutor.

If you are on a budget and cannot afford a private tutoring service, there are plenty of independent tutors, including college students who are proficient in Wonderlic subjects. You don't have to spend thousands of dollars to afford a good tutor or review course.

We wish you the best of luck and happy studying. Most importantly, we hope you enjoy your coming years – after all, you put a lot of work into getting there in the first place.

Sincerely,
The Trivium Team

CPSIA information can be obtained
at www.ICGtesting.com
Printed in the USA
BVHW050832130222
628620BV00004B/397

9 781635 307016